JOB INTERVIEW QUESTIONS AND ANSWERS

By
Jim Barret

Jim Barret

DISCLAIMER

The information contained in *"Job Interview Questions And Answers"* and its components, is meant to serve as a comprehensive collection of strategies that the author of this eBook has done research about. Summaries, strategies, tips and tricks are only recommendations by the author, and reading this eBook will not guarantee that one's results will exactly mirror the author's results.

The author of this Ebook has made all reasonable efforts to provide current and accurate information for the readers of this eBook. The author and its associates will not be held liable for **any** unintentional errors or omissions that may be found.

The material in the Ebook may include information by third parties. Third party materials comprise of opinions expressed by their owners. As such, the author of this eBook does not assume responsibility or liability for any third party material or opinions.

The publication of third party material does not constitute the author's guarantee of any information, products, services, or opinions contained within third party material. Use of third party material does not guarantee that your results will mirror our results. Publication of such third party material is simply a recommendation and expression of the author's own opinion of that material.

Whether because of the progression of the Internet, or the unforeseen changes in company policy and editorial submission guidelines, what is stated as fact at the time of this writing may become outdated or inapplicable later.

This Ebook is copyright © 2019 by *Jim Barret* with all rights reserved. It is illegal to redistribute, copy, or create derivative works from this Ebook whole or in parts. No parts of this report may be reproduced or retransmitted in any forms whatsoever with the written expressed and signed permission from the author.

Jim Barret

Table Of Contents

INTRODUCTION 1
A TYPICAL JOB INTERVIEW PROCESS 2
HOW TO MAKE A GREAT FIRST IMPRESSION 5
TYPES OF JOB INTERVIEWERS 13
    How do you tackle this then 17
    Different Types of Interview 18
    How to Be Successful in Different Types of Job Interviews 20
    Things You Must Do Before a Job Interview 23
WHAT EMPLOYER'S WANT IN TODAY'S COMPETITIVE JOB MARKET 25
    What Do Employers Want From Their Employees 32
    What Employers Need To Hear 33
    Soft Skills That Helps You Stand Out And Impress Hiring Managers 34
    Ten Things Hiring Managers Look For In Job Interview Candidates 37
DIFFERENT TYPES OF INTERVIEW QUESTIONS 42
    99 Common Interview Questions And Answers 45
    The Difficult Questions 70
    Mistakes to Avoid When Answering Tricky Questions 77
    To Ask Or Not to Ask 81
    Questions to Ask the Job Interviewer 83
    Tips For Acing A Job Interview 85
JOB INTERVIEW MISTAKES TO AVOID 93
    Avoid These Ten Mistakes 93
    Finish Strong! 100

INTRODUCTION

Thanks for choosing this book, make sure to leave a short review on Amazon if you enjoyed it, your opinion is very important for us!

You've searched for job openings, you found a few businesses that you like, and you've filled out a few job applications. You may have also sent in a resume and cover letter. For all of your efforts, an employer has contacted you and would like for you to come in for an interview. This is where most people start sweating or at least get a little scared.

When you are looking for a job, preparing to go through a series of job interviews can certainly be a stressful experience. One thing that can put your mind at ease the next time you have a job interview scheduled is to look at the interviewing process from the eyes of an interviewer as this will help you get a better understanding of how the interview process works.

Preparing for job interviews is something that you may not think too important, but most of us get to our first interview - the first in years perhaps - and lack of planning becomes fairly obvious. With a job interview where you really are excited about getting a job offer, this can be hugely disappointing, and the chances are the interviewer has planned well and knows what they want to hear and what they are looking for. Given how much time and effort you need to put into getting the interview it makes sense to ensure that you give yourself the best possible chance of success at the actual interview

A job interview is an opportunity for the prospective employer to learn more about your skills and qualifications for the job and to determine if you would be a good fit for the organization. Also, it should be a job that meshes with your career plan.

A job interview should not be an interrogation. When going on a job interview, you need to understand that this is going to be the first impression your potential employer will get of you. It is important that you dress properly for the interview and this means always wear business attire. Even if the job you are applying for is casual, you want to make a good impression with this employer.

A Typical Job Interview Process

So you have decided to search for a new job, great! But what do you do now? Listed below are several steps outlining and preparing you for the job interview process.

Update Your Resume

Your resume is your selling point. All the employer has to look at and consider is what is listed on your resume. Make sure your resume is too the point, informative, relevant, and up-to-date. Make sure all of your references are aware they are references, your contact information is accurate, and your name is spelled correctly! Lastly, make sure you used an organized, professional format.

Submit Your Resume

Now that you have updated your resume, it is time to submit it. You can submit your resume directly to a company, or you can use a job board. Both are beneficial avenues to pursue. Keep in mind, you should always submit your resume to multiple companies at the same time, this way; if one doesn't work out, you already have another one lined up. Having choices will help you take the stress away from the job interview process.

Check Back With Potential Employer

If it has been more than two weeks since you submit your resume, a friendly e-mail or phone call may benefit you in multiple ways. It shows persistence, interest, initiative and helps inform you as to where you are in the process.

Receiving the Phone Call

Once an employer has viewed your resume and has taken an interest from it, they will contact you via e-mail or phone to schedule a phone interview. While not every company chooses to pursue a phone interview, multiple companies do. Make sure you start practicing!

Phone Interview

On average, a phone interview lasts between fifteen minutes to an hour. These questions are used for pre-screening purposes. To view a list of possible phone interview questions, click here.

Phone Interview Callback

You should receive a callback no more than a week after the phone interview took place. However, things can happen. If you don't hear back within a week-and-a-half, be sure to contact the potential employer. If you did receive a callback, it was to schedule a face-to-face job interview.

Live Interview

You made it to the face-to-face job interview! Congratulations. Now make sure you don't mess it up! Make sure you dress properly, combed your hair, cut your fingernails, researched the company, and practiced your response to possible interview questions.

Live Interview Feedback

When the phone rings, don't get nervous! Remain calm and sound confident. At this point, the employer will ask you to agree to a background check or tell you, "We don't have a position that will fit you now, but we will keep you in mind should something come up." It may hurt, but it's not the end of the world, remember, you did apply for multiple jobs!

Background Check

This is the easy part. They look you up and inform the employer as to whether or not you are who you say you are. Some checks go back more than ten years so make sure you are open if you know something they don't!

Offer

So long as you passed the background check with flying colors, the employer will come back to you with a position and salary offer.

Counter-Offer

If the offer is everything you imagined and more, great! If not, or even if you want to try to get a little more, make a counter-offer. Don't be too greedy, and don't sound too desperate!

New Job

If everyone is happy with the offer on the table, then consider yourself a new employee of that company! Hooray!

How to Make a Great First Impression

Your appearance, style, fitment in the team, and even your possible future success quotient are all summed up in the first impression that you create on the interviewer.

Considering the importance of these factors in a job interview, you would hope that you're given sufficient time to make a great first impression, but this is not to be.

Three seconds, expert research says that this all you have to make or break an impression that has a significant impact on the outcome of your job interview.

Job interviews last almost an hour and often get into specifics mentioned on the resume, so why bother about the first three seconds?

That's because while your education and experience are important, they are not the only deciding factors. Today most jobs also leverage the personality of their employees to support and generate business. An impressive personality will be a better team player, and an approachable individual will make a better manager; with longer work schedules and increasingly stressful workplace environment, pleasant employees definitely help soften the blow.

Research indicates that an individual's personality is reflected in one's overall appearance. Accordingly, first impressions that are created in approximately three seconds can be used as a good indicator to gauge an individual.

Interview applicants are many, and interviewers greet the above research finding as it makes their work easy - if the first impression doesn't impress, move on to the next candidate.

So keeping in tune with the popular saying that well begun is half done, here are some simple ways to make a positive start to the all-important job interview.

Punctuality

You have to be on time unless the reason is more important than getting the job. Even in that case, call and either reschedule or inform that you would be delayed.

Always remember to confirm the location with the recruiter, plan ahead and familiarize yourself with the route. Know what transport you will take and if you're planning to drive, budget some time for parking.

Plan to be at the interview location 30 to 45 minutes early. If there are unexpected, unavoidable delays always call to inform. It is rude to keep people waiting without informing them, and you don't want to lose the job even before you get it.

Dress Well

A casual approach is best reflected in your clothes. The corporate world categorizes attire into Business Formal, Business Casual, and Informal - know the difference and pick options from Business Formals. Your clothes must be well laundered, ironed and sober; also pay attention to self-grooming (nails, hair) and wear a mild fragrance.

It is always better to dress up than to risk dressing down. The interview is important to you, so show that you want to make a great impression. There's no harm in letting your attire say "I'm going for an interview"; there is a problem; however if it says, "This is just another day."

Your interviewer will make an assumption as to what type of person you are when you arrive, and they will make this assumption within the first few seconds of you walking through their door. This is important.

Dressing smartly doesn't have to mean dressing like everyone else - if you want to show a little bit of your personality, and it's the right environment to do so, then add a bright color under that suit or a subtle piece of jewelry. Your attitude to work, and of course to the interview itself, can be read by what you are wearing and how you hold yourself so dressing to impress can mean thumbs up or down at your interview. Interviewers want to feel that you have taken their job and their company seriously and taking time over your dress and general appearance goes some way to giving them this assurance.

We always try to dress for the job that we want, so if you want to be the next Marketing Director or Stylist, dress in the way you would expect them to and let a little bit of your personality out!

You also need to ensure that you are comfortable in the chosen outfit. So wear it around the house a bit, practice sitting and getting up (in front of the mirror). You do not want to look like this is the first time you have ever dressed like this!

Radiate Confidence

Show that you're prepared with a firm handshake and a confidently toned voice. Sit upright in the chair to radiate self-belief and eagerness.

Remind yourself that you've done your homework and are prepared for even the toughest of interview questions. Your confident actions will silently communicate to the interviewer that you're the best candidate for the job and you're there to get it.

Smile

Definitely refreshing for others, a smile will also quickly relax your own nerves. Note that going overboard with unnecessary giggling could be misinterpreted for foolishness, immaturity or even flirting.

If smiling does not come to you naturally, take some time to practice it in front of a mirror. You may feel awkward doing so, but smiling is a powerful tool and owning it will benefit you in all walks of life.

Remember to complement a good smile with fresh breath.

Be Positive

The best interview advice anyone can give you is to remain positive - about yourself, your views and of course your last employer/s. If you left your favorite job because you and your manager clashed, then you might not want to go into detail instead preferring to say you left to find similar work which was better paid, or that you wanted to find a more career-minded company, or you wanted a new challenge. Things like this don't need a mention, but of course, you will normally be asked why you left a role or why you took on a particular job. Think positively, and this helps you shine at your interview.

Remember to stay engaged during the interview conversation, nodding your head and maintaining good eye contact are sure ways to impress.

Body language is a very transparent mode of communication, and expert interviewers frequently use it to pick up clues about the interviewee; know the signs that you are sending out through your gestures.

Always be honest but be circumspect at the same time - this is not a counseling session but a job interview. Remember also that the interviewer will have in the back of the mind that this is how you will talk about them and their company in the future.

Courtesy Sir

Treating others with respect is the mark of a dignified individual. Remember your greetings and include the liberal use of 'please,' and 'thank you' in your conversations.

Some people may tell you not to be overly formal, but there is no such thing as excessively formal. As a caution, while giving respect to others, remember to not short sell or underestimate yourself.

Preparedness

Commuting to the location may ruffle your hair or work up a sweat; carry accessories that will perk up your appearance and your mood. One of the most common mistakes is forgetting to carry a pen and a pad to take notes.

A great way to ensure that you are fully prepared is to have a couple of mock interview sessions where you behave as if you are going to the actual interview. It is more effective when you have someone who can play the part of the interviewer and ask you some potentially tough questions.

Making a great first impression is must in every job interview, and trying to do that can sometimes become a nightmare. But remember that preparing for an interview is a systematic process and by following the simple checks mentioned above, you can be sure that you are prepared and confident for the big day in your professional life.

Have All Appropriate Documentation

Before your interview ensure that you have several copies of your up-to-date CV, a copy of your letter of application (or the application form you completed). It is also common for companies to request that you bring additional documents with you on the day of the interview such as identification so make sure you read your letter of invitation carefully before the day of your interview.

Switch Your Mobile Phone Off

This may seem like an obvious point to make but it is surprising how many candidates forget to do this (perhaps due to nerves) so make sure that you are not one of these people by turning your phone as you arrive at the interview building.

Maintain Good Posture & Eye-Contact

Your body language is extremely important during an interview, so try to focus on maintaining a good posture (avoid slouching even if the interview is conducted in a casual manner). Look the interviewer in the eye when responding to their questions but remember to glance at other members of the interview panel from time to time during your answer (this will demonstrate confidence and awareness).

Listen Carefully & Think Before Answering

Interviewers are aware that they may be asking particularly probing questions and therefore expect you to listen to their question carefully

Jim Barret

and take a moment or two to answer them so take advantage of this fact and take your time to make sure you answer their exact question in a concise, clear manner.

Types of Job Interviewers

As you prepare for a job interview, it is quite important to note that you will be facing an interviewer who will make a decision about your presentation. It is equally important to know that the interviewers also come in different sizes and shapes and that they are all different from the other. Some of the general types of interviewer you might face include the following

The Pedant

They are interested in knowing your level of experience and technical knowledge. Will torment you with a stream of technical interview questions. The main aim is to get you to either to a state that you do not know or catch you out.

You better understand your technical know-how about the job you are being interviewed since it will be clumsy for you to be employed as an accountant yet you know nothing about contingent liability.

Most pendants are line managers or functional heads who have a vacancy that needs to be filled. They want to be certain that the positions get the best technical resource possible.

The Obnoxious Type

This is the rude, interruptive type who will want to belittle you during a job interview. Sometimes the rudeness could be well calculated as a hostile interviewer to observe your reaction when under pressure. This kind rarely listens to your response to the end. Could be very irritating.

The Nice Guy

This is a charming interviewer who will even thank you for attending the interview in the first place. The nice guy will make you comfortable via a small talk with the hope that he/she will be able to know you better when you are calm and relaxed.

However, sometimes this type of an interviewer could be placing you in a comfort trap and then pounce on you with a barrage of questions.

The Parent

This interviewer cuts across a parent figure to the interviewees. They will offer an encouraging smile, will nod in approval to a correct answer and will appear quite supportive. This may be done to achieve one of the following; either to help you put your best foot forward which is pretty nice or, to lull you into a feeling of security to the point of letting your guard down.

The Observer

Ever been to an interview and then noticed the interviewer who never uttered a single word throughout the session but just kept a gaze on you? This "observer" type could be the company's decision maker and are out just to observe how you respond to the interview questions throughout. They will finally recommend you to be employed or not. Be wary of them and treat them with respect.

The Disorganised

A very annoying type of interviewer of course. This will have papers strewn all over the table in the interview room, may not even have read your CV, can't find your application, may not know your name or even more irritating, may know nothing about the job position being interviewed.

Most likely this type on interviewer could have been picked that morning and asked to interview you on behalf of someone else or could be a typical case of an overworked line manager who had even forgotten about the interview.

Just remember you are seeking the job and not him/her. Try to impress upon that you are the right talent.

The Know All

These interviewers believe that they are God's gift to humankind and won't hide that fact from you during the interview. Their sense of overconfidence and tremendous ego is very visible.

They come across as very effusive, aggressive, highly opinionated, oppressive and bigoted.

Always believe they know exactly what is required of a candidate and that they have an unerring eye for picking the "right candidate".

They are bullies and will not settle for a job candidate who seems to be a threat to their confidence. They are always looking for "boot lickers" in job searchers.

The Chauvinists/ Bigots

Trust my word; there are bigots out there in the world of interviews and job search. They believe women should be in the kitchen, or that a carpenter's son should be in the woods.

They believe everything on earth is pre-destined and no one can change that. This one will outrightly show discrimination depending on the bias he/she hold about a job candidate.

Always learn to remain focussed and mature and respond to questions posed to you devoid of bias.

The Lost One

Could be the funniest of all. This kind will always appear in a panel interview. He/she will sit and just listen to what other interviewers have to say. Then from nowhere, they will interject with a very irrelevant question to the silence of everyone else. Always remain focused in the face of such an interview tragedy.

The Insecure Interviewer

This is the sheepish type of interviewer possibly suffering from inferiority complex. They always have a feeling that there is an area beyond them that they should not be interviewing.

You will always notice their nervousness which could worsen your already tense situation. They rarely make eye contact, can't keep still on the chair, fidget with pens and papers, divert to unrelated topics, have a structured list of interview questions beyond which they cannot ask anything else. They will also agree with nearly everything you say, ask you to repeat information you had already given and may only ask interview questions that need only a "yes or no" response.

This type could be line managers who have risen through the ranks because of their technical competence while ignoring soft skills training.

How do you tackle this then

Remember you honored the interview since you wanted to clinch the job and nothing else. Therefore;

- Always give the interviewers enough information concerning self to prove that you are the best-suited job candidate.
- Always corporate and show that your team skills are pretty smart.
- Learn to keep calm and patient even in the case where the questions are repetitive.
- Remain diplomatic and tactful even when you feel irritated.

Different Types of Interview

Face-to-Face interview

This is the most common and traditional type of interview. Generally, one to one conversation is there. The interviewee should maintain eye contact, and his answer must lead to prove that his qualifications are best suited for that job.

Panel Interview

Generally more three to ten members can be in the panel of interviewer interviewing the candidate. Candidate needs to adjust with the personalities of the panel as soon as possible maintaining proper eye contact to all the interviewees.

Behavioral Interview

The interviewer asks questions to predict your behavior. It can be related to your history; all you need to do is to give answers based on facts not only hypothetical activities.

Case Interview

The interviewer wants to know your problem-solving potential. He/They may give you a situation or a case, and you are supposed to give a logical solution to that. It should be noted that only solution does not matters but the approach, how you apply your knowledge is important.

Telephonic Interview

This is conducted for screening purpose, or we may call it a preliminary interview. In case when the interviewer can not conduct face to face interview for all the applicants shortlisted for an interview due to some limitations. For this kind of interview, one must ready for any time interview and the phone on which call is to be received must be trouble free (No call drops, network problem or call waiting kind of problems). Preferably one should choose a landline.

Group Interview

It is an informal discussion type of interview. The employer judges the leadership potential of the employee and the way he interacts with the group.

Mealtime Interview

This is conducted for jobs which require interpersonal activities. The interviewer judges how you would react in a social gathering. You need to be confident, well mannered, and follow the lead of the interviewer.

Stress Interview

In some professions, you need to tackle a lot of stress and thus stress interview becomes important for this kind of job. The employer wants to know your reaction in stress. The interviewer may be sarcastic; he may open challenge you believes or may ask you to do any insulting activity, etc. So you have to be calm and tactic and do not take questions personally, it is a game. Try to answer logically in a positive manner.

Jim Barret

How to Be Successful in Different Types of Job Interviews

Let's go over the various kinds of employment interview surroundings to ensure you will be able to get ready and what exactly to anticipate from each and every one.

Telephone Interview

This is the 1st step in a job interview procedure. It's an assessment technique. It is best to be equipped for this kind of interview by recalling the following guidelines.

Have a cheat sheet next to the telephone. Always keep a listing of your positive results handy as a note of the topics you would want to cover.

Look for a quiet spot to have the telephone dialogue.

Stand-up when talking, this certainly will supply your voice additional power. Also, it will make it appear more confident. You need to understand this is a conversation, restrain from consuming food, drinking, and chewing gum.

Be involved in the conversation. Demonstrate curiosity by answering with a "yes" or "I see." Demonstrate determination in your speech.

Panel Interview

This employment interview manner will involve three or more people who are going to be interviewing the potential candidate concurrently. This interviewing approach is mostly used when submitting an application for an opening in the education or government industry markets. To scale down the amount of pressure give thought to the following pointers.

Obtain business cards from each participant of the panel interview whenever possible. Place them on the table in front of you in accordance with their placing; this will assist you in memorizing their names.

Resolve each question to the best of your potential. Take into consideration that you are able to answer one question at the same time hence be very inclusive in responding to your questions. Maintain your eye contact with all members of the panel when answering an inquiry.

Behavioral Interview

The main purpose behind this form of job meeting is to make the interviewing process as honest as possible. The questions in the behavioral interview process are fashioned by a psychologist with a purpose to recognize distinct personality types.

The interviewer possibly will write down or record your responses. Carefully consider the contributions you have made in your projects history mainly where there is a significant or noticeable change.

Situation Interview

During this kind of job interview, a workplace is artificially generated. This means you are most certainly needed to commit a certain amount of time in the place of work. In mostly all conditions your work will be watched by a group of individuals.

The main purpose of this is for the employer to get a good idea of how you would react in particular work situations. It is possible that you may be asked to solve hypothetical problems related to particular work procedures, or even give a presentation.

The situation interview helps the interviewer in observing whether the candidate actually possesses the required skills and work experiences the company demands.

Meal Interview

This is a less formal procedure for employers to evaluate potential employees. Here are some helpful tips for meal interviewing.

You will probably be asked to order first. Don't change your mind on the food item once you've ordered. This will make you look indecisive.

Order dishes that take a middle position in the price range, and are not "sloppy foods."

Try to avoid alcohol. If drinks are ordered politely decline or "nurse" a drink.

The purpose of the job interview from the company's perspective is to find something that fills their needs. An interviewers job is to be able to asses how your background and skill set can help the company meet its goals and objectives. Job hunting is a competitive environment, therefore, developing a good way to effectively present your abilities and expertise will obviously put you ahead of the pack.

Things You Must Do Before a Job Interview

There are things which one must do to get himself prepared for a job interview. One of the factors which make many people not to do well in the job interview process is procrastination. Unfortunately, lots of people have not been able to overcome the problem of procrastination and other drawbacks to the job interview processes. Here are the tips that can make a difference in the job interview processes.

1. The first thing you need to do is to have a deep look at the job you are applying for and try to fashion out how you will address the need of the employers. Look out for the specific needs of the organization and find the answer to all their needs; this will position one to be a candidate to beat in the job interview processes.

2. There is this popular acronym that is called TODAY which stands for Teamwork, Overcoming the Obstacles, Duties of the previous positions, Achievements, as well as Your strengths and those that you can call your weaknesses. It is proper to put what you did in each peculiar situation; this will make the employers have a balanced judgment about you.

3. The other useful tip is to carry out research about the company which interview you are planning to attend. Search can be done

through the internet. Make a visit to the website of the organization and study what they stand for and have an idea of what the worker the company is hiring can do for the organization. This will put one in a better position to do well in job interviews.

4. The other important factor to consider is to develop the type of question that you are going to ask the interviewer. This can be done by having a look at the job post and fashion out two to three intelligent questions that you can ask the interviewer if the time for those approaches. Always look at the line of their products and the type of projects that they engage in, and ask intelligent questions that are relevant to their types of products.

5. The final stage is that you have to be well prepared to provide the answers to the various questions that would be put to you. Always have answers for such questions at hand, questions like providing necessary information about yourself, reasons why you left the previous job you were doing, the reason why you think that you are the best material that can be hired for the job, and also the question that may crop up about salaries and remunerations. You have to be well prepared for the answer for that type of questions when they arise.

What Employer's Want In Today's Competitive Job Market

1. Patience

Employers can sense desperation a mile away because most job candidates apply with just getting the job in mind. Most job seekers are neither strategic nor intentional in putting their best foot forward. The way you ask questions during an interview or the way you follow-up after you first contact employers tell them everything they want to know about you. If you call back a week after they said to wait two weeks, or if you're asking the same questions several times then you'll fail their character test.

2. Personality

Most companies can't train great characters. It's hard for them to find qualified job seekers with required skills and a personality. If you want to stand out and be memorable, show a smile, ease, responsiveness, and a little humor (appropriate and family friendly). It's not just the way employers make you feel, but what companies experience with you after you leave.

3. Proactive

If you are networking with people in a company you want to work for, you should be learning what makes the environment tick. Then you can use the information to include on your resume and to bring to the interview to impress employers. If you don't know anyone, you should use resources such as Glassdoor or a LinkedIn Forum to see if you can gather more intelligence. Another way is to find out what the competition is doing when interviewing with other companies.

4. Honesty

In the news, we have seen every level fail in showing transparency and honesty even in the application phase. If you can prove your accomplishments through social media, or testimonies, you will immediately stand out to employers. But even without proof, your body language, actions, and speech will vouch for your integrity. References and testimonies about your work make this your most powerful tool. If you don't have any recommendations on your LinkedIn profile, make it a priority because it is the best place to show it's a real person who is testifying about your work.

5. Resilience

Part of your career story should include how you were steadfast during challenges in mergers and acquisitions, changes in leadership, withstanding a hostile culture, or how you handled disappointment. There are some managers who ask about how someone's job search is going and sift out those who complain about the way other employers handle the interviewing process. Businesses measure character as an essential part more than ever. You can show them you are steadfast in cultures requiring you to pivot constantly.

6. Quick And Perpetual Learner

Showing you're a perpetual student also says you're coachable and teachable. And for some jobs it's everything. It costs employers a lot of money to train and if you can shorten training because you quickly absorb information will make you valuable. If you are positioning yourself to talk about your accomplishments and results such as, "I learned this system in this XXX time which is X% ahead of schedule."

7. Persistence

People are drawn to individuals who are persistent especially when coupled with enthusiasm. Where it matters is after meetings and interviews and follow-up without being annoying. Usually, employers will define for you what they consider boring and what is respectful. Monitoring is essential to your job search, and persistence is a needed element to achieve results. Furthermore, it impresses employers with the right amount of patience.

8. Courage

Showing you're unflappable during changes impresses employers. Courage is associated with leadership and rarely disappoints. Part of your overall career story should include a narrative where you were willing to do something no one else volunteered to do. Not that you needed attention on you but in seeing the bigger picture, there was a need. It is not found how much or volume but in how significant and what it made others feel.

9. Perseverance

"How do you manage stress" is often asked by employers. It answers comes in all shapes and sizes but best displayed in stories, and it's better when validated by others. Every company would love to hire a persevere-at-all-cost employee, but examples through storytelling make your case.

10. Purpose

A person who has personal reasons to serve and desires to make a difference owns fundamental reasons to excel. It is a rare attribute to drive a career, but it makes a job candidate pretty attractive when accompanied by the right set of skills.

Employability skills, also known as key competencies or soft skills, are those basic skills necessary for getting, keeping, and doing well on the job. These are the skills, attitudes, and actions that enable workers to get along with their fellow employees and supervisors and to make a sound, critical decisions.

Employability skills are divided into three skill sets: (a) necessary academic skills, (b) critical thinking skills and (c) personal qualities. The three skill sets are typically broken down into more detailed skill sets.

Familiarize yourself with these skills and ask yourself where you may need improvement:

- **Basic Skills**

These skills are the foundation of your career building blocks. The ability to read with understanding, also known as reading comprehension is critical to successful employment. If you cannot fully understand the instructions on how to apply for a job, you are at a disadvantage.

Many jobs require reading as part of the duties. There are reports, memos, emails and safety requirements that are part of the day to day functions of the job. Poor reading skills will cause you to lag behind other workers because it takes you more time to understand and interpret what you are reading.

Employers look for people who communicate well both orally and in writing. You need communication skills to sell yourself during the interview. Being able to convey your thoughts both verbally and in writing helps you to be understood by your coworkers. Excellent communication means better relationships in the work environment. Listening skills involve not only hearing but understanding.

The sign that you were looking is that you can act on the information that you heard. Looking means gaining information and understanding information. Math is also part of making decisions and reasoning. Basic math skills are used in the workplace when purchasing and ordering supplies, following a budget, or just managing your vacation time.

- **Critical Thinking Skills**

Critical thinking skills involve decision-making and problem-solving. The ability to make decisions is also an asset to an employer. Decision making and reasoning include gathering information, evaluating a variety of solutions, and selecting the best option. You can save your organization time and money by demonstrating these skills.

People with these skills are particularly useful in customer service positions. Perhaps you solve a problem with an angry customer that allows them to be satisfied and continue supporting your employer.

The abilities to problem solve and make well thought out decisions are critical to any workplace.

Planning and organizing are also critical thinking skills. The ability to plan and organize means you will get the job done and done correctly. A person who is well organized is prepared to do the job correctly the first time.

Creative thinkers come up with new ways of doing things that add value to the work environment and serve customers more efficiently. They offer new perspectives about the job and the company. Finally, a lifelong learner is always a valued employee. Employers know that to stay ahead of the competition they have to learn new and better ways of doing things. The person who is open to learning new things is going to be more successful than the individual who is afraid of learning new things.

- **Personal Qualities As Skills**

Leadership is the ability to influence others toward the achievement of a goal. Leaders have self-confidence. Leaders are team players. Team spirit is an interpersonal skill that allows individuals to work together to achieve the best results for the employer. They exhibit social skills by respecting the thoughts and opinions of others. It makes for a peaceful work environment.

Self-management or self-control is the ability to manage your personal feelings and reactions to challenges on the job and in life. Personal grooming is a part of self–management. A good employee is well-groomed and well-dressed because he or she knows that their appearance is a reflection on the organization.

Self-management can also include things that you do that are not linked to a particular job, something as simple as being on time, responsible, cooperative, or motivated, or have a positive attitude. No employer wants to spend his or her day settling office disputes or watching the clock make sure an employee uses time wisely.

Employers want to hire workers who are honest and can manage themselves in these areas. Some jobs involve change on a daily basis; therefore, employers want people who are adaptable, flexible, and patient and respond well to change. Employers look for these skills to help to determine how a candidate will fit into the organizational culture.

- **Technology Skills**

Discussing employability skills would be incomplete without discussing technology. You can't escape the use of technology today. Whether it's using your debit card at the grocery store, the ATM at the bank or the self-check-in kiosk at the airport, technology is present. More and more employers require that employees become familiar with a wide variety of computer applications. Computer literacy is knowing and understanding not only what computers can do but also what they cannot do.

Even if you are aware that you will not be using the equipment on your job, it is well worth your while to at least introduce yourself to this form of technology. The Internet is loaded with tools that will assist you in finding a job, keeping a job, and advancing in a job. You can also meet and learn from all sorts of people from around the world through social media. If you have your computer with an Internet connection, you can access information at all hours of the day or night, at your convenience.

To be technologically literate, you need skills in these areas: exchanging e-mail, browsing the Internet, and using Microsoft Word and Microsoft Excel.

What Do Employers Want From Their Employees

Employers want employees who are dependable, trustworthy, and good at their jobs.

Great employees share certain characteristics, and these are the ones that companies seek above and beyond the ability to fill a job description. If you are looking to position yourself as a great employee, make sure you recognize the six valuable characteristics below that employers' look for when hiring, say our experts.

Employers want employees who demonstrate dependability. Certain core expectations are required for all jobs, but dependability is probably at the top of the list. Employees show reliability by taking personal ownership of all aspects of their job, including being on time, dressing and working in a professional manner, and demonstrating a high level of commitment. Managers like dependable employees because they set and maintain clear expectations.

Job Interview Questions And Answers

What Employers Need To Hear

Employers want employees who are self-motivated. While the role of every manager is to motivate staff, they appreciate and seek ones that create their motivation. It makes a huge difference to have an employee that has an inner drive to organize their work versus one who needs constant guidance to perform day to day activities. Employers look for employees that have a level of self-motivation that will not require a high level of "hand-holding," as well as the ability to tackle the expected obstacles that arise in day to day business.

Employers want employees who provide a positive representation of their brand. Employers seek individuals that will enhance their organization and their brand. They want to recruit people who are trustworthy, have solid reputations inside and outside of work and have a good work ethic. Great employees have a strong sense of what is appropriate in the workplace and outside, and they know how to balance the two.

Employers want employees who rise to the occasion. A good employee gets the job done. A great employee gets the job done in spite of everything including when priorities and schedules shift. They are self-motivated and can problem solve and think on their feet.

Employers want employees who are team players. No one can achieve "greatness" in an organization completely alone, and remarkable employees know this to be true. They are the consummate team player who can highlight their successes, as well as praise others for theirs. These employees recognize that success is better achieved through teamwork, always.

Employers want employees with a positive attitude. Great employees maintain a positive attitude, even during stressful situations. They tackle projects, both big and small, in a straightforward manner.

Soft Skills That Helps You Stand Out And Impress Hiring Managers

Degrees and credentials are important, but the development of soft skills skills that are more social than technical are a crucial part of fostering a dynamic workforce and are always in high demand. Have you taken inventory of your soft skills set? You may have skills that are high in demand and now even know it.

We have all gained skills from past jobs, responsibilities, life experiences and interests. You may even have hidden skills that, when identified, can be added to your resume and help you to become a better contender in your job search.

What Are Soft Skills?

Soft skills are general skills like the ability to accept feedback, work collaboratively, manage your time, etc. These are skills that will help you in a wide range of jobs, not just the target job you're applying for.

Here are the top ten soft skills in demand for today's job market:

1. **Communication Skills**: It's more than just speaking the language. Communication skills involve active listening, presentation as well as excellent writing capabilities. One highly sought-after communication skill is the ability to explain technical concepts to partners, customers, and coworkers that aren't tech savvy.

2. **Computer And Technological Literacy**: Almost all jobs nowadays require basic competency in computer software, but many job seekers fail to provide this section because they think it's implied. If computer skills are relevant to your field, insert a "Technical Skills" or "Systems Proficiencies" section to your resume.

3. **Interpersonal Skills**: The ability to work in teams, relate to people and manage conflict is a valuable asset in the workplace. This power is necessary to get ahead and as you advance in your career, the aptitude to work with others becomes even more crucial. Personal accomplishments are important on your resume, but showing that you can work well with others is important too.

4. **Adaptability**: Don't underestimate the ability to adapt to changes and manage multiple tasks. In today's technology-driven and rapidly evolving business environment, the ability to pick up on new technologies and adjust to changing business surroundings is necessary. Display your relevancy in the

workforce by referencing an example of how you adapted to a sudden change at work in your resume.

5. **Research Skills**: With Google at the tip of your fingers, it's easy to find answers to common issues. However, hiring managers seek employees that are skilled at assessing situations, can explore multiple perspectives and gather more in-depth information.

6. **Project Management Techniques**: Organization, planning and implementing projects and tasks for yourself and others is a highly useful skill to have. In the past, this was a job in itself. Nowadays, many companies aren't hiring project managers because they expect all of their employees to possess certain characteristics of this skill.

7. **Problem-Solving Skills**: The ability to use creativity, reasoning, experience, information, and available resources to resolve issues is attractive because it saves everyone at the organization valuable time. Highlight this skill by listing an example of when your organization had a sticky situation, and you addressed it.

8. **Process Improvement Expertise**: The number one goal every company has in common is to save money. Optimizing business procedures can save a company time and money. Quantify results in your resume by listing the before and after facts of projects that you took on.

9. Strong Work Ethic: Employers are looking for employees that take initiative, are reliable and can do the job right the first time. Managers don't have the time or resources to babysit, so this is a skill that is expected of all employees. Don't make the hiring manager second-guess by sending a resume with typos, errors and over-exaggerated work experience.

10. Emotional Intelligence: Although you will most likely never see this in a job description, EI is a highly sought after skill that relates to your social skills, social awareness, and self-management abilities. Emotional intelligence is usually something that is revealed through actual interactions with the hiring manager, but you can hint that you have it with a strategic resume the addresses areas where your experience and skills are lacking about the job requirements.

Ten Things Hiring Managers Look For In Job Interview Candidates

Job Interviews are much like auditions, and often it is the excellent performance that gets the gig. However, not everyone is cut out to provide a stellar performance in the pressure chamber of an interview. Even for the best candidates, a moment in the spotlight can give them a sense of stage fright.

The first lesson in nailing an interview is to know exactly what hiring managers look for in a candidate. Yes, there can be hundreds of details from wardrobe choices to resume format and a nervous applicant could quickly bog down with any one of them. Keep in mind the old saying, "don't sweat the small stuff."

Sticking To The Basics, And Improve Your Chances Of Getting The Job.

In preparing for a career-making audition, a few things should certainly top the list. Ten things hiring managers to look for:

- **Can You Do The Job?**

Not surprisingly, the entire hiring process rests on this simple premise. Can the candidate do the job? In the excitement of making this far in the recruitment process past the initial application, telephone screening, and resume submission-many candidates fail to ask themselves this fundamental question. Carefully examine the requirements of the position it should be part the preparation for the interview and be prepared to explain clearly how you can do the job.

- **Are You Who You Say You Are?**

An effective resume tells a story of past accomplishment, education, and strengths; it does not reveal who you are. The interview is an opportunity to rise above a piece of paper (or electronic file). If a resume is inflated, embellished or puffed-up, it will become apparent in a face-to-face meeting. In sales, the cardinal rule is "never overpromise and under deliver." The interview is the same.

Studies have shown that potential for the future trumps past accomplishments when judging a candidate for a job. Expressing confidence and the sense of "the best is yet to come" could be enough to get a candidate over the top, and into the position.

- **Are You A Good Fit?**

Every company has a way of doing business, beyond what is in the employee manual commonly referred to as "corporate culture." If you are a comfortable person, then you might have difficulty in a formal suit-and-tie office. It is like forcing an oval peg in a round hole; it is close, but not enough to be ideal.

For many job seekers, a casual atmosphere would be a welcome change of pace, just make sure you can perform in that environment. Again, researching the company before meeting with the hiring manager is critical to identifying the corporate culture.

- **Are You A Team Player?**

Collaboration is a skill that is necessary; responsibility rarely rests on someone who cannot work well with others. It also plays into the corporate culture will a candidate's unique style overshadow the expectations of the team or will their contribution elevate the entire group? Mavericks may have a role in the office, but without the support of others, it could be a conflict that could lead to problems.

- **Can We Trust You?**

Skills and experience are the key traits in a new hire, but trust (or the lack of it) can be a quick deal breaker. Is a candidate trustworthy and believable? Hiring managers look for the right person, someone they can depend on to perform the job functions or conduct the business. Even the best jobs have involved, difficult or even mundane tasks; employees must be relied on to fulfill those tasks, no matter what. Of course, it takes the time to build the groundwork for trust, but in the interview, the first impression of trustworthiness is crucial- without it, your chances are zilch.

- **Communication**

The applicant has to be able to appropriately and clearly communicate with co-workers, site managers, and customers, among others. Having instructions get misstated, or be unclear, can negatively impact your business. A candidate must be able to concisely communicate instructions, safety information, deadlines, and budget restrictions when necessary. Confusion on the job site, or in the office, can lead to possible added expenses and injuries.

- **Time Management**

Sometimes at a construction site, or on a line in a factory, an employee may be left unsupervised for extended periods of time. When this happens, you have to know that they are making the most of their time on the clock. If they are not very good at prioritizing their tasks and managing their time, they could end up wasting most of their time rather than utilizing it. It can run into budget issues, deadline problems, and production issues. It can throw your schedule off for completing a job on the building site.

- **Problem Solving**

Problems will always pop up when you least expect them. From running out of nails, to a machine breaking down, to another employee not showing up for work there will be days where if something can go wrong, it will. Knowing that you have an individual in place who can take care of those problems can give you peace of mind and open you up to applying your time and attention to other important issues.

Hiring someone who can cover another employee's shift, who can find additional nails to finish up a particular project, or who can get your project fixed in an expedited manner will be someone you will be glad to have to work for your company.

- **Passion For The Job**

If you have an employee on a construction site, or in the design office, who is not passionate about their line of work, you could be missing out on a valuable input source. Someone who knows the details of their career can offer opinions on helpful updates, innovative ways to do things, and safety suggestions. They can also help train other employees as needed, and they can turn out to be a valuable part of your team. Passion for the job can lead to a happy employer and an even more happy employee.

- **Business Aware**

Not only does the ideal candidate have a passion for their field of expertise, but they are also aware of the business aspects of the field. Understanding that there is more to the job than just getting it done it has to be done right, on time, and on a budget is an important quality to look for in a candidate.

Different Types of Interview Questions

Companies utilize a set of interview questions as a tool to analyze the qualities of a job applicant for a certain position required by the company. These questions are specifically designed to thoroughly get substantial information from an applicant to know whether he is qualified for the job. Interview questions are also used to validate the information contained in the applicant's curriculum vitae or resume.

An interviewer prepares a set of interview questions which he asks all applicants. He will then compare the answers given him and gauge from here who the most qualified applicant is. It is the human resource department who usually prepares these questions. And they have set a standard set of answers also to measure the qualifications of every applicant.

Interview questions vary depending on the company's preference and needs. There are no standards or patterns in these types of questions. Basically, there are different types of interview questions which job applicants may encounter during interviews. These types of interview questions have their specific objectives pertaining to the different qualities of the job applicant.

Credential Authentication Questions

This type of interview question aims to gather enough information on the applicant's previous background. The common question includes "How long have you worked at the company?"

Work Experience Questions

These types of questions aim to evaluate job applicants' working experience with previous employers. It raises questions related to duties and responsibilities performed with the previous work.

Work Competency Questions

The most common questions with this type include, "Could you provide examples of your qualities as a leader?" or "Elaborate on how you have provided solutions on certain problems in your work?" The main purpose of this type of question is to measure the behavior and the competency of the applicant which can contribute to the position being applied for.

Opinion Questions

In some cases, interviewers would raise opinion questions to see how an applicant responds to certain scenarios. The interviewer usually provides an example scenario wherein he will ask questions like "If you encountered this problem, what would you do? What are your strategies?" In this type of question, the interviewer may ask the applicant on his or her strength and weaknesses.

Dumb Questions

Some interviewers use dumb questions just to test the applicant's ability to think instantly. This type of question does not have any right or wrong answers. Some of the common questions used are "What is the color which represents your personality?" "If you were given a chance, what animal do you like to be, and why?"

Mathematical Questions

Mathematical questions are given in order to measure the mental quickness of the applicant. It also evaluates the ability to formulate a mathematical procedure. It also measures how alert an applicant is in mental thought processes.

Case Questions

Case questions are designed to rate the problem-solving capability of an applicant in certain situations. Examples of questions used include "What is your forecast with regards to online retailing?" or "How many gas companies in the European region?"

Behavioral Questions

This type of question is usually used by many companies. Most companies give greater importance to the behavior of their applicants rather than the skills because they believe that an applicant with good behavior can be trained in terms of skills. It is basically designed to predict the future behavior of an applicant by basing it with its past behaviors. Questions used with the interview include "Give specific experiences of how you have handled such situations. What are the specific steps you have implemented in order to finish the task?"

Thanks for choosing this book, make sure to leave a short review on Amazon if you enjoyed it, your opinion is very important for us!

Job Interview Questions And Answers

99 Common Interview Questions And Answers

Although it can be difficult to know exactly which questions to expect during your interview, here are some of the most commonly asked interview questions? Write out your answers, remembering to focus on how your accomplishments would benefit the company. Then, either conduct a mock interview with a friend, practice in front of a mirror, or videotape yourself answering the questions. The more practice you get, the more poised and confident you will be.

1. How do you handle non-productive team members? The Best way to handle a non-productive team member is to envision how they can be productive. Usually there is a reason for their non-productivity and often they will reveal it to you personally or sometimes you may have to probe for the reason simply by asking them a question "What do you like most or least about working here?"

Once you have isolated the negative problem, suggest solutions that are the easiest to obtain in the shortest period. Research suggests positive reinforcement is the best way to motivate a person. Share a story about "seeing the light at the end of the tunnel" that you experienced personally.

It will help develop more rapport and enable trust from the "non-productive team member." Positive reinforcement includes primarily reinforces such as smiles, touch (handshakes), verbal thanks and mutual support such as talk about payday, bonuses or potential promotions for achieving or exceeding goals. Share the positive vision.

2. How do you motivate team members who are burned-out, or bored? A bored team member is simply not challenged enough. They are being satiated (doing a task for too long of a period). In this case, switch jobs for a short time or pair them up with another team member to shorten the boring task. See if it's possible to give them more challenging work if they complete the boring task first.

3. How do you handle team members who come to you with their personal problems? Contrary to public opinion, a person that comes to you with a personal problem trusts you to help them. Trust allows you to get people to do things you want them to do. Share a straightforward, and quick answer (a similar situation that you may have personally experienced) then suggest doing a productive task at work that will distract them and provide personal achievement that they are not getting in their home life.

4. What are your career goals? How do you see this job affecting your goals? My goal is to acquire an IT position that utilizes my talents more efficiently while increasing my flexibility in scheduling tasks. IT jobs are moving towards home office utilization to save company costs and travel time. This IT position will allow me to save on transportation time (to and from work, lunch and dress preparation) therefore I can work on new programs and creative ideas without the typical corporate distractions.

5. Explain how you operate inter-departmentally. Two words that best describe me are "Chameleon liaison." I can change and adapt to my environment in seconds since I have worked in various departments over the years. My understanding of each agency's needs allows me to convey information precisely. The shorten communications via phone, email and in person minimizes frustrations and allows me more time flexibility to delegate or to take on more complex tasks.

6. Tell me how you would react to a situation where there was more than one way to accomplish the same task, and there were hard feelings by others on each position. First of all, I acknowledge the posts regarding the work. I break down the missions in a Ben Franklin fashion with Pros on one side and Cons on the other. After reviewing both sides, I recommend taking a consensus vote to confirm the pros outweighing the cons.

7. Consider that you are in a diverse environment, out of your comfort zone. How would you rate your situational leadership style? My leadership style is democratic or consultative. I believe in gathering differing views to gain a consensus. In particular, I discuss group thinks principles where teams tend to take the view of the person of authority even to the detriment of the team. By letting the group know that their opinions have no sanctions and that every idea benefits the group through discussion.

8. Give me an example of your leadership involvement where teamwork played a significant role. Interestingly a leader isn't always leading when it comes to collaboration. When I worked in a sales

capacity trying to close a deal, I allowed other members to discuss various other topics unrelated to the sale at hand. The customer wasn't ready to close the transaction because the trust wasn't established yet. Members of my team were better suited to discuss personal topics allowing me to do calculations and revisions to the quote.

9. Tell me about a situation where your loyalty was challenged. What did you do? Why? Commitment is achieved through trust. A lack of engagement means that you trusted someone with too much information or a task to perform. When it's not obvious to the other person, I mention the hardship that it caused and remove a positive reinforcer such as money or status with the option for the individual to regain the loss after proving their worth. The reason for removing a reward is not to accidently continue rewarding the wrong behavior.

10. In what types of situations is it best to abandon loyalty to your manager? As James's Groupthink theory suggests a group may go along with a manager's decision even though they all know it's to the detriment of the team. Another reason to abandon loyalty is if your manager is engaged in illegal or misconduct that you may eventually become a party to the action.

11. In today's business environment, when is loyalty to your manager particularly important? All the time except in cases of misconduct. Loyalty is of particular importance to gaining position or to make future changes to your business climate. If you don't show your trust in someone else, why should they trust you?

12. Why are you interested in this position? I am interested in this post because my skills allow me to do the work required with minimal or no training required. Also, I enjoy this job because of the freedom and creativity I can add to the result.

13. Describe what you think it would be like to do this job every day. I realize that some days will be challenging because of the short deadlines. However, I do my best work under pressure -always have. Based on my experience working for the competition I expect my days to be very similar except my skills being put to better use.

14. What do you believe qualifies you for this position? In addition to my challenging experience, I differ from other candidates because I have started up experience. I have the drive to initiate and complete an assignment with minimal outsourcing.

15. What have you learned from your failures? In a nutshell, I learned a multitude from my failures. I have learned that you should hire outside of your friendships and family because they both parties often can't distinguish business from their personal life. I've also learned to outsource the tasks that I'm not adept at solving. More than anything, I've learned that many successful people have failed more than once but what makes them a failure is quitting. Failure's without quitting is just a part of a platform of character building.

16. Of your previous jobs, which one did you enjoy the most? What did you like the most/least? Why? What was your major accomplishment? What was your biggest frustration? I enjoyed my

own business the most. The main reason is that I had total flexibility in providing the level of customer service my clients requested. Most companies have several people doing several tasks for clients; I was able to handle all of those tasks with a single point of contact for the customer.

What I liked least was handling the financial responsibilities. Only, I'm not cut out to deal with mundane tasks of record-keeping, as a creative specialist, my talents are best suited dealing with creative tasks and outsourcing what I'm not good at.

17. Tell me about special projects or training you have had that would be relevant to this job. I have worked with hundreds of clients across the spectrum of social, economic status. My ability to relate to the shipping clerk is just as useful as discussing growth options with the CEO. Moreover, I can link information as a liaison between departments.

18. What are some things that you would not like your job to include? I would not like my job to put me into morally compromising positions that not only jeopardize my Karma but would infect the entire company's reputation as a world leader. I also would not want to take unsubstantiated financial risks that may have devastating consequences to our labor force.

19. What are your current work plans? Why are you thinking about leaving your present job? I don't ever think of myself as leaving a position. I work with hundreds of clients; they are all my bosses from

time to time. As I assume this post, I am doing so because of what I can do for my client(s). I did excellent work for my past clients, and I'm moving onto more challenging tasks where my new customers can benefit from my experience. My current work plan is to get up to speed with these organizations policies and procedures of excellence.

20. Describe an ideal job for you. An ideal job is where I can ask all the questions needed to assess a problem, task and solution accurately. Also, positions, where I can listen and have people hear in the most efficient manner possible, are highly desirable.

21. What would you do if you found out that a contractor was in a conflict of interest situation? I am usually the person that finds out this kind of information. First, you have to evaluate how much of a conflict there is. Many times situations have mutual benefits, and you need to know exactly what's involved, but as soon as I have enough information I bring it to a supervisor or superior in confidence.

22. If I were to contact your former employee, what would he say about your decision-making abilities? Here is his phone number, email, address, and website. He has written my recommendation letter specifically outlining my decision-making skills. Those include price control, purchasing, hiring, time management and prospecting. He usually tells people that if he is not available for the job, then I'm the next person to call.

23. Give me an example of a win-win situation you have negotiated. I took on a project where the client wanted a repair but said the

replacement would not be adequate but would pass inspection. I suggested utilizing an old product for an area and then using a new product that would cost the same amount of money as the initial repair cost. The client got more than he asked for and my job was completed quicker saving me time and money a win-win.

24. Tell me about your verbal and written communication ability. How well do you represent yourself to others? What makes you think so? My oral and written communication style are to engage the client with enthusiasm. I know my style is effective simply as a result of recommendations and referrals I receive. I set goals to receive one referral for every three clients on average.

25. Give me an example of a stressful situation you have been in. How well did you handle it? If you had to do it over again, would you do it differently? How do you deal with stress, pressure, and unreasonable demands? I was given a task to complete a proposal within hours without any knowledge of the software and particulars of the client's requests.

I completed the assignment on time using a combination of three software packages. I would have done it differently with one software package, but I had to try three until I found the proper fit. I perform well under stress, so that wasn't a problem. However, I did suggest to my supervisor that a particular software package worked better than the others and that it should be used as our standard. I also asked if that in the future I could be given more time to complete an assignment by staying later the night before or being able to come in sooner.

26. Tell me about a tough decision you had to make? I had to separate my personal life from my business life by not working with family members. Even though there are many advantages to working with family the disadvantages outweighed the pros.

27. Describe what you did at your job place yesterday. I prepare my daily list of tasks to be done for the day. Using outlook, I set reminders for priority tasks and add to them as they come in via requests. That way I don't miss functions, and I keep proper time management. I went to two clients and gave proposals and immediately sent thank- you letters via email for the opportunities. I continued to work on projects according to my task list.

28. How would you solve the following technical problem? (Describe a typical scenario that could occur in the new position.) A client called about their computer being locked up. I usually follow a format to do a full reboot (not a restart). I monitor the client over the phone to log in, as usual, to make sure the computer is no longer locked up. I also follow up with some questions on what programs were open so that they don't cause usage problems.

29. What strengths did you bring to your last position? I brought tenacity, perseverance, listening skills and a sense of humility for others.

30. Describe how those contributions impacted results? By being tenacious, I continued to ask questions and clarify the objectives, so our team didn't waste time putting together a proposal that didn't hit the

mark. With perseverance, I continued throughout the night making sure we had met the morning deadline.

Most people spend their time talking and never learning anything. I make a special effort to listen to the requests which made the presenter feel more comfortable with choosing us as a provider. I often ask how a person is feeling about an issue so that they feel my empathy. It builds rapport and confidence that I/we can handle bigger and more challenging tasks.

31. What are the necessary steps to successful project management?
- Ask questions to clarify objectives.
- Verify that you are on target.
- The complete task on time.
- Ask for follow-up work or have signed punch list.
- Bill or Invoice project

32. How do you plan for a project? First I research any items I'm not certain about. I verify who all the players are and what their schedules consist of. I check my schedule to see if there are any conflicts. I make sure I have all the materials and necessary expenses to accomplish the task(s) on time.

33. What is important to consider when planning a(your type of project)? It is important to find funding, time management, and potential accolades or future business opportunities.

34. What are things that you have found to be a low priority when planning for (your type of project)? Typically transportation and lunch considerations are of low priority. They can help and are necessary, but they tend to be things that can be put off as the work completion takes precedence, then the time it takes and how to get somewhere for lunch or dinner can wait.

35. What distinguishes a project from routine operations? Operations are daily events that don't differ significantly from day to day. A project, on the other hand, has specific goals and differing methods of accomplishing them.

36. What are the three constraints on a project? Three typical constraints on a project are time, funding, & technology.

37. What are the five control components of a project? There are five control components to every project:
- ❖ The control environment,
- ❖ Risk assessment,
- ❖ Control activities,
- ❖ Information and communication, and
- ❖ Monitoring.

38. What qualifications are required to be an effective project manager? The skills of a project manager are that they be good communicators. They need to communicate regularly with the project team, as well as with any subcontractor. Efficient and frequent communications are critical for keeping the project moving, identifying

potential problems, and soliciting suggestions to improve project performance. It will keep customer satisfaction and avoid surprises.

A high level of communication is especially important early in the project to build a good working relationship with the project team and to establish clear expectations with the customer. The project manager needs to create clear expectations of the members of the project team, so everyone knows the importance their roles are regarding the project objective.

The essential qualities of the project manager are strong leadership ability, ability to develop people, excellent communication skills, good interpersonal skills, problem-solving skills, and time management skills.

39. What experience have you had in project management? I have handled hundreds of projects from quoting/estimating, designing, installation and service.

40. Name five signs that indicate your plan may fail. 1) Poorly defined scope. 2) Loss of executive sponsorship. 3) A change in business needs. 4) Funding. 5) Labor choice.

41. Tell us about a project in which you participated and your role in that project. We had a new software release. My job was to make sure that batch jobs were submitted on time and that they were generating the proper reports. Also, I had to make sure that the data was being back up and mirrored correctly for onsite and offsite storage.

42. When you are assigned a project, what steps do you take to complete the project? I create an accurate check off list for each milestone. Once I complete each task I send off an email to the corresponding parties and any action they have to take as a result. After checking their responses, I add new tasks or modify the work to stay on target. Once the project is complete, I send the similar reports through the proper channels.

43. As you begin your assignment as a project manager, you quickly realize that the corporate sponsor for the project no longer supports the project. What will you do? I will research to see if I can get another sponsor for the project and speak with my supervisor to discuss our alternatives.

44. Your three-month project is about to exceed the projected budget after the first month. What steps will you take to address the potential cost overrun? First, I will find ways to shave time and therefore the cost of the overrun. I will also consider outsourcing some of the work to lower costs via a bid process. I will put together the necessary additional funding request to my supervisor.

45. Tell us about a successful project in which you participated and how you contributed to the success of that project. I worked on a new rollout where each team was responsible for separate sections of the development. My task was to act as a liaison between the teams to make sure the project was completed on time. If a team were falling behind, I would find additional work members or ask the team if I could help reduce their time expenditure.

46. You are given the assignment of project manager, and the team members have already been identified. To increase the effectiveness of your project team, what steps will you take? I will by democratic vote ask each team to identify a leader. I will stay in contact with the head of each team to make sure he or she has the resources to complete the task on time.

47. You have been assigned as the project manager for a team comprised of new employees just out of college and "entry-level "consulting staff. What steps can you take to ensure that the project is completed against a very tight time deadline? I will ask each employee what their strengths and weaknesses are so that I can pair the most knowledgeable members with a less knowledgeable member to balance the group evenly.

48. What is a "project milestone"? A milestone is the end of a stage that marks the completion of a work package or phase, typically characterized by a high-level event such as completion, endorsement or signing of a deliverable, document or a high-level review meeting.

49. What is "project float"? Project Float: the cushion you provide yourself b4 committing a date to customer. Suppose your planned schedule completion is: 15 June, and you promise the customer 15 July for completion of deliverables, you are giving yourself a month more time.

50. Your project is beginning to exceed budget and to fall behind schedule due to almost daily user change orders and increasing

conflicts in user requirements. How will you address the user issues? I would discuss the reasons for the daily change orders and see why those are happening. Probably the objectives have not been clearly stated, so changes are being made to the project as they are being clarified by each team member.

51. You've encountered a delay in an early phase of your project. What actions can you take to counter the backlog? Which actions will have the most effect on the result? Take a look into the delay and see what's happening. Isolate the reason for the delay such as technical problems, team problems or an individual. The best bet is to work with each and help them solve their efficiency problem. Set in place a monitoring schedule perhaps a tracking program with screen shots or regular emails showing a chronology of progress.

52. Describe what you did in a challenging project environment to get the job done on time and budget. On one particular project, I had to stay in constant contact with the vendor to make sure the product was being completed on time.

It included checking estimated delivery schedules or to check and sign off on design reports moving through the engineering dept. I usually tried to keep a fixed price schedule, so I didn't go off budget. If the vendor was late, they have to pay associated fees for being late.

53. What actions are required for successful executive sponsorship of a project? Know and communicate the business goals, put accountability in the right places and get people excited.

54. How did you get your last project? Through a BNI (Business Network International) B2B group.

55. What were your specific responsibilities? I was the education coordinator. My job was to present our company and do presentations on our service. We also shared networking strategies with new and existing members.

56. What did you like about the project and dislike about the project? I liked the flexibility of doing most of the project from home. The budget for the project was thin so I didn't profit as much as I would have liked, but sometimes you have to take a few low-budget projects with new clients to get the better paying projects.

57. What did you learn from the project? I learned how to research particular products and present them mixing and matching marketing materials from different vendors.

58. Tell me about a time when you ran into any stressful situations. How did you handle them? Delivery timelines were changed by the client after the job was accepted. I had to modify the parameters of the project so that the customer could use 75% of the project and get the other 25% of the project as regularly scheduled.

59. Tell me about the types of interaction you had with other employees. Different employees have different impacts on a project. If they were involved in the presentation to the client, then we brainstormed the best method to communicate with the customer.

Other employees involved in delivery were notified of potential changes and updated on completed product.

60. Tell me about an accomplishment you is especially proud of and what it entailed. I worked on a project that I never worked on before. I went to a trade show and found a couple of vendors that produced a similar product. Using their marketing materials and cost sheets I had another vendor reproduce their product at a lower cost and thereby increasing profit significantly.

61. Do you have people from your past consulting services who would provide a professional reference? Absolutely. ABC Contracting Rick Berzowski. Mike Hintz from Classic Cargo International. George Tzortsos from G.E. Medical/Kohl's Department Stores.

62. What other similar consulting or independent contractor services have you rendered? I provide specialty technical writing onelance.com.

63. Discuss how you would envision working as an independent contractor or consultant for us. I have a working history, portfolio, and reviews.

64. What different responsibilities will you have? I will not have any different responsibilities. I can set my freelance schedule as I see fit. This position will take full priority over any other project. Much like any home life by freelance schedule is akin to a personal hobby.

65. What would be your specific goals for this new role as a consultant or independent contractor? My specific goals are to accomplish each and every request on time and in the budget. I look forward to building my portfolio and my success with this company is paramount.

66. What experience do you have that you think will be helpful? My particular experience as Owner or operator of a commercial dealership and a co-owner ship of a service company makes me uniquely qualified.

67. This assignment will require a lot of (describe). Will that be a problem for you? Discipline is necessary for these types of projects. My past has given me the fortitude to complete assignments on time. Not only will this not be a problem for me, but it will also be a pleasure.

68. This assignment will require interacting with (describe the types of people). What experience do you have working with such people? I have experience working with various consultants and IT professionals. Working as a Computer Operator and Help Desk Analyst, I have worked with Networking Analysts, Programmers, and IS Directors.

69. What would you like to gain from this new assignment? More than anything, I'd like to gain the satisfaction of having others depend on me for the profitability of the company.

70. What are two common but major obstacles for a project like this? What would you do in the face of these barriers to keep your team on

schedule? Time and communications are the major obstacles for this project. Constant communications with clear cut goals signed by each member is a start. Also, I recommend using positive reinforcement for achieving milestones.

71. What is project charter? The Project Charter details the project purpose, overview, goals, and high-level deliverables. What are the elements in a project charter?

The project overview- A project overview contains a description of the business need, purpose, and product or service that is to be provided.

72. Which document will you refer to for future decisions? I would use the Contract.

73. How will you define scope? When the project was proposed for funding, there should have been an initial set of objectives and deliverables defined. There may even be some high-level scope statement.

Any information that was created earlier should be used as the starting point for identifying the more detailed scope statements. If you find that you do not have enough information to create a clear and comprehensive scope statement, you must work with the sponsor to gather additional information. That is the purpose of the definition and planning process.

One place to look when defining scope is the project objectives. By definition, there need to be one or more deliverables created to accomplish each goal. Looking at the deliverables then becomes the basis for the scope definition. After you determine what major deliverables the project will produce, start asking other questions to determine other aspects of range.

The deliverables describe 'what' the project will deliver. You can also identify 'what' organizations are impacted, 'what' types of data are needed, 'what 'features and functions are required, etc.

74. What is the output of the scope definition process? As a point of clarity and contrast, you can also identify out-of-scope conditions by describing what deliverables will not be created, what organizations will not be impacted, what features and functions are not included, etc. Of course, there are an infinite number of out-of-scope statements.

For scope definition, you want to include only those statements that help define the project boundary and touch upon related areas that the reader may have questions about. For instance, if you were installing financial software, you might state that a new Accounts Payable package is in scope, but the related Purchasing System is out of scope.

It is a good practice to document those organizations that are in scope and those related organizations that are out of scope. The readers can then determine more quickly if they are impacted or expected to assist in the project. Also, it may make sense to identify what organizations are in scope so that you can have people from those organizations represented on the project team - perhaps on a Steering Committee.

75. What is quality management? An ongoing effort to provide services that meet or exceed customer expectations through a structured, systematic process for creating organizational participation in planning and implementing quality improvements.

76. Do you inspect or plan for quality? Every project should have a quality program. In reality, very few do. You can see that if you were checking project quality, you would have an inspector who would typically be external to the Project Team

77. What is EVM? How will you use it in managing projects? Earned Value Management is a management methodology for integrating scope, schedule, and resources, and for objectively measuring project performance and progress.

78. What is a project? And what is a program? A project is a temporary endeavor undertaken to create a unique product, service or result. The temporary nature of projects indicates a definite beginning and end. The end is reached when the project's objectives have been achieved or when the project is terminated because its objectives will not or cannot be met, or when the need for the project no longer exists. A program is a planned sequence and combination of activities designed to achieve specified goals.

79. What are project selection methods? Project selection methods are defined to show the project is 'worth' taking it. Strategic goals of the organization, Market Need, Technological Advancement, Competitive Advantage, Profitability, Project/Portfolio Management Office (PMO), and Sponsors are critical in project selection.

80. Which tool would you use to define, manage and control projects? I would use the Project/Portfolio Management Office (PMO).

81. What is risk management and how will you plan risk response? The process of determining the maximum acceptable level of overall risk road from a proposed activity, then using risk assessment techniques to determine the initial level of risk and, if this is excessive, developing a strategy to ameliorate appropriate individual risks until the overall level of risk is reduced to an acceptable level.

The plan is frequently applied in the project management software as a series of tasks in addition to those that were on the original activity list. The risk mitigation plan may also identify specific triggers, which are events that spur action based on the escalating proximity of a given risk. As risks become imminent, the risk mitigation plan identifies what actions should occur and who is responsible for implementing those actions.

82. What are outputs of project closure? Project closure is the last phase of the project life cycle and must be conducted formally so that the business benefits delivered by the project are fully realized by the customer.

Did it result in the benefits defined in the business case? Did it achieve the objectives outlined regarding reference? Did it operate within the scope of the mandate? Did the deliverables meet the criteria defined in the quality plan? Was it delivered within the schedule outlined in the project plan? Was it delivered within the budget described in the financial plan?

83. What are the methods used for project estimation? The three methods for project evaluation include equations, comparison, and analogy.

84. What methods have you used for evaluation? I have used the estimation methods using equations.

85. How would you start a project? I would put together a project plan.

86. If you were to deliver a project to a customer, and timely delivery depended on upon a sub-supplier, how would you manage the supplier? What contractual agreements would you put in place? I would handle the provider by making sure they sign the contractual arrangement. A standard buyer and seller agreement would be a start. Other methods can be obtained through a lawyer.

87. In this field (the field you are interviewing for), what are three crucial things you must do well as a project manager for the project to succeed? The three critically important things to do is create the features list, goals list, and work items list.

88. What metrics would you expect to use to determine the on-going success of your project? I would utilize cost, effort, & duration as my primary metrics.

89. How are your soft skills? Can you "sell" the project to a team? As a sale professional, you must find the customers buying motives. Once you have identified their reason for buying, you can isolate their objections and provide solutions.

90. You have a team member who is not meeting his commitments, what do you do? I would try and motivate the team member by setting a more achievable goal. If they cannot make that goal then I would consider replacing the team member.

91. Companies have historically looked at technical skills, but more and more business managers realize that not having "people" skills tends to cripple projects. I agree.

92. How many projects have you handled in the past? Deadlines met? On time/ within budget? Obstacles you had to overcome? I have managed approximately 25 projects. Most of the deadlines were met, and most customers were willing to extend the deadline.

93. Do you understand milestones, interdependencies? Resource allocation? Yes.

94. Do you know what Project Software the new company uses and is there training for it? The software was indicated on the company

website. Other social media sites have reported the company has training and professional development.

95. Tell me about yourself. (To avoid rambling or becoming flustered, plan your answer.) What differentiates me from other project managers is my entrepreneurial enterprise. With extensive knowledge of pricing and product value on a multitude of manufacturers, I can competitively position products against or within a client's inventory to adequately assess their needs. If there is a phrase that best describes my talents, it would be "creating something out of nothing.

"Whether I'm working with the A & D community on new space or creating an ergonomic, product, or design standard for companies with a variety of existing products, I create customized functional solutions below budget expectations developing long-lasting quality relationships.

96. What are your strengths? (Make an exhaustive list and review it exhaustively before the interview.) My strengths include Fortitude, Humility, Creative, and Perseverance or Industrious.

97. What are your weaknesses? (What you say here can and will be used against you!) My weakness is a tendency to be a perfectionist.

98. How would your current (or last) boss describe you? My current boss has told me that I am invaluable and indispensable.

99. What were your chief's responsibilities?(Interviewers sometimes ask this question to prevent you from having the chance to claim that you did your boss's job. Be ready for it!) My boss's position is to run and operate the company's finances.

The Difficult Questions

Being invited to an interview is half the battle. That means you have already impressed the potential employer with your CV showing your work experience, skills, and educational history. He or she has already read about your background. The interview is the opportunity to get to know you as a person and to evaluate your compatibility with the company. During the interview, you will be presented with many difficult questions, some you have never considered before. To ease your nerves, prepare yourself by taking some interview help.

Many people make the mistake of entering an interview expecting to regurgitate what the employer has already read on your CV. You would not be asked about your work history, but rather more personal questions. Rather, you would be asked such questions as "Tell me about when a project went wrong," "How do fire an employee?", "What do you do when two members of your team cannot work together?", "Where do you see yourself in 2 years?", "Why did you apply to this company?" Most of the difficult questions asked in an interview have underlying intentions. These questions will test your nerves, honesty, and ability to work under pressure.

Every employer wants honest employees. The interviewer will attempt to pry as much information from you as possible to get a feel for your personality and honesty. Since that is the interviewer's agenda, be yourself and be honest in the interview. When presented with questions about your personal character, answer with confidence and relate your answers to your prospective job's objectives. You will probably also be asked about your previous or past job. When answering any of these questions, especially the questions directed towards why you left or what you enjoyed least about the job, stay professional and answer honestly without demeaning your previous or past job. Do not point blame at the company, rather explain why you felt you were not a good fit for the company, and follow with some qualities of the company you are interviewing for and why those suit you better.

The interviewer knows you are nervous. In the workplace, no matter how nervous you are, you must always maintain your professional composure. In an interview, there's no such thing as an innocent interview question even if you're asked by an assistant on the way to or from the interview room! Depending on the organization, the ten popular interview questions below might be asked in a slightly different way, but the motivation behind the questions is the same. Interview preparation will ensure that you always have a good interview answer to hand.

Q1. What have you been up to since you left your job?

Saying, 'I've had a chance to catch up on all the chores to do around the house' is not a good interview answer. An organization wants to employ people who are energetic, self-motivated, and determined. The longer you have been out of work, the more important it is for you to show that you have managed your time well. This might mean volunteering for work where you can use your skills and abilities, attending courses so that you upgrade your skills, and being active in a business or professional network.

Q2. How long have you been looking for a job?

Unfortunately, it is true that the longer you are out of work, the more difficult it is to be offered a job, and you lose interview self-confidence. With this popular interview question, the potential employer wants to know whether there something wrong with the candidate that has been out of work for a long time. When there's a chance that you might be 'out of work' for a considerable time, it is important to give yourself a deadline and then consider taking a job which might be a contract position or a job in another area of the country. Even consider a job where you're overqualified. All jobs at every level can be used to promote a candidate so don't feel that taking a job below your qualifications means that this will be held against you in the future. Being seen as a pragmatist and a hard worker will help you to stand out against the competition for a job.

Q3. Why do you want this job?

This is a very popular interview question but saying, 'because you saw the advert is not a good interview answer,' even if it's true. It's a buyers market, and a potential employer wants to employ a person who is keen and enthusiastic to work with them. If they find a candidate who's genuinely interested in their company, then they believe that they're more likely to stay and succeed in the new job. The candidate who prepares for the interview by reading up on the organization and demonstrates an understanding of their strategy, management team and current issues is more likely to capture the interest of the interviewer. Find something specific about the company that complements your own experience and ambitions. It is even more impressive if you've 'gone out of your way' to understand the organization such as talking to other employees or their customers.

Q4. What do you consider to be your greatest achievement?

In an interview, candidates tend to smile and nod a lot. The potential employer is interested in getting to know the 'real' you and whether you're going to fit within the culture and role of their organization. Asking about your achievements is a popular interview question. The achievement you choose to talk about says a great deal about you and your personality. A good interview answer is to choose an accomplishment that relates to the position you're applying for. If this isn't obvious pick an accomplishment that required some of the same strengths that will be needed for the job, if you're applying for a leadership position in a task goal orientated culture then the interviewer is going to be impressed by someone who is motivated by achieving a project or goal and inspires others around them. In an entrepreneurial organization, a 'creative mind' will be more appreciated. The ability to 'think on one's feet' will be considered critical to a high level of success within their organization.

Q5. What salary did you earn in your last job?

Companies will frequently find different ways to ask an interview question to determine the candidate's salary requirements. Your last salary is a good way for them to determine whether they can afford you. If the salary the organization is offering is considerably lower than your previous salary, they'll have concerns over whether you will stay in the job. If this is the case, then a good interview answer is to convince them that you are prepared to live on a lower salary and why. Sometimes, companies will ask the candidates, 'what salary do you require? If this is too high for their budget, they will look at other applicants. A good interview answer is to say that you are willing to start on a lower salary with bonuses driven by targets. This gives them savings on their budget and a safety net if the candidate does not achieve as well as expected.

Q6. What do you think is your weakness?

One of the most important tasks of the interviewer is to find a candidate who they would like to work with and who is likely to get on with other people in their organization. Candidates often try to answer this popular interview question with a positive trait disguised as a weakness. For example, 'I'm a bit of a perfectionist' or 'I tend to work too hard and expect others to do the same.' An interviewer is looking for someone who has a level of maturity and self-awareness as this is an important trait for creating empathy and working with people. To stand out from other candidates a good interview answer is to mention a genuine weakness, and then emphasize what you've done to overcome or manage your weakness. This is evidence of a truly confident person who takes personal responsibility for themselves.

Q7. Your experience of working with someone difficult?

By asking this popular interview question, the interviewer is acknowledging that we can all have a problem working with people some of the time. This is a popular question for revealing any prejudices that the candidate might have. Today it is essential that an interviewer employs a candidate who is comfortable working with people from a diverse range of ethnic, cultural, ages and religious backgrounds. A good interview answer would be to mention a specific person who you found difficult to work with rather than a group of people. Give a specific example such as a person resisting change on one project. Importantly, demonstrate the difficulty and how you resolved the issue.

Q8. What will you be doing in five years?

Ambition and drive are great qualities in a candidate as it demonstrates energy to persevere and reach goals even in tough times. However, an organization also wants to see signs of stability and loyalty to employers. If your CV shows that you've moved every eighteen months or so the interviewer is likely to need reassuring that you're not going to 'jump ship' to a competitor in a year from now. A good interview answer is to talk about the opportunities you've researched within their organization and your ambitions to excel within it, particularly if you can refer to employees within their organization. Setting Clear Objectives before you go for an interview is useful; otherwise, you can waste time applying for jobs you're unlikely to get.

Q9. Why are you the best person for the job?

As with answering all the other popular interview questions try and appear confident and likable. A poor interview answer is just to say that you're better than any of the other candidates. You don't know the qualifications or experience of the other candidates! A good interview answer is to focus on three to five specific reasons why you should be hired and briefly substantiate your claims. Remember, to tell the interviewer that you're really enthusiastic about being offered this job and determined to demonstrate the contribution and value you can make to their company. Knowing how to sell yourself is an interview is a very great interview skill.

Q10. Is there anything you want me to ask you?

Many firms now ask a similar open-ended question. This is not a trick question but just gives the candidate a chance to speak on their own behalf. If you think that there have been any problems in the interview, this is your chance to go back into an area which you think the interviewer may have doubt about you. It is not a good interview answer to say, 'no' as this can show that you're not interested in the job. It can also give you a chance to reiterate a strength which you think is important and might distinguish you from other candidates.

Mistakes to Avoid When Answering Tricky Questions

When it comes to a job interview, blunt and poorly phrased answers may spoil your chance to get hired. More often than not, interviewers throw tricky questions with the intention to identify certain personality traits or generic skills they are looking for.

Wouldn't it be good if you can know their intention in advance? How to avoid common mistakes in answering tricky job interview questions? Can you tell them exactly what they want to hear so that you get hired?

Here are five tricky job interview questions and the mistakes you should avoid when answering them. Find the sample answers and improvise them to suit your own career experience.

Tricky Question 1: What did you like and dislike about your previous job?

It will be a big mistake if you try to tell them that your previous job was perfect or a total disaster. If it was perfect, the interviewer might think that you will not find the job you are interviewing for as satisfying as the last one. Avoid using high pay or lots of vacation days as you like.

On the other hand, if you say it was a total disaster, it may be viewed as negativity in personality. You need a good mix of likes and dislikes. Avoid the dislikes that you are likely to face in the job you are interviewing for.

The interviewer is trying to judge your behavioral competency through this question. Some examples of how your last job provided the opportunity for you to flex your expertise will be good. As for the dislikes, you can mention things that are beyond your control. Casually say that the dislike you mentioned is not a big problem for you and give your view on how they could be done better.

Tricky Question 2: Give me an example of a problem you faced in your previous job. How did you solve it?

You may be very capable, and many problems seem insignificant to mention. However, it would be a big mistake if you tell the interviewer that you have never faced any problem in your previous job (even if it is true). Avoid answering this question with general and high-level answers such as the number of cases you have handled in your previous job or the total cost you have saved for your previous company.

The interviewer is trying to judge your problem solving and critical thinking skills. You should use this opportunity to share specific cases where you solved problems effectively and creatively. Highlight the major root cause of the problem (e.g., technical, teamwork/relationship, budget/cost).

Explain the steps you have taken to solve the problem. It will be a big plus if the cases you share relates to the job you are interviewing for.

Tricky Question 3: What have you learned from your past mistakes?

Big mistake if you say you have never made a mistake! Be brief in answering this question an avoid offering too many negative examples too. Avoid faulting other people when talking about your mistake.

The interviewer is trying to see if you have the maturity it takes to examine your own mistake and learn from it. It will be good if you offer an example to show that you take responsibility for your mistake and that you have been successful in correcting it.

Tricky Question 4: Describe a situation when working with a team that produced more successful results than if you had completed the project on your own.

It will be a big mistake to say that you have to capability to work alone and do not require the help from the others. Avoid saying that you can't function independently too.

The interviewers are trying to find out your ability to work in a team. You can offer some examples whereby you participate effectively as a member of a team. Highlight how you have listened and accepted ideas from others or persuaded others to your point of view.

Tricky Question 5: Describe a time when you were faced with problems or stresses at work that tested your coping skills. What did you do?

Don't pretend that you never get stressed out in your previous job. Avoid saying that your previous job is very relaxing.

The job that you are interviewing for is likely to be very stressful if this question is asked. Most importantly, don't be stressed up. Stay calm during the interview.

The interviewers want to know your approach in dealing with stress. Let's face it. Most jobs are stressful. Share with them how you avoid stress through planning and time management. Exercises and spiritual activities are great too.

By avoiding the mistakes in answering tricky job interview questions, you have effectively kept your chance of being hired alive. Of course, you need more than that to get hired. The key to success is simply to prepare well. Do your homework. Write down the key points in answering the tricky questions and common questions. Find out exactly what the hiring manager wants to hear during the interview. (This will be discussed in other sections of this book) That will gain you an unfair advantage over the others.

To Ask Or Not to Ask

The most common notion about job interviews is that the interviewer is the one asking all the questions while the job applicant should just sit properly on the chair, and answer all the questions the interviewer throws. True, right? Well, if you are one of those many people who still believe this, it's about time to throw that belief away because nowadays, job interviews are more than just a one-way street. If you are scheduled for an interview or expecting a call to be interviewed, it would really help you if you have prepared some job interviews questions and practice how to answer them.

Asking Signifies Interest

It is a pretty obvious fact that interviewers or potential employers ask job applicants a lot of questions for two reasons: first, they want to get more information from the applicant and second, they are interested with what the applicant has to offer.

With that same logic, it would just be perfectly fair if the applicant also asks job interviews questions to their potential employers. By doing this, they would not be only narrowing their doubts and skepticism with regards to the company; they would also be giving themselves an edge because asking questions during an interview would give off an impression that an applicant is interested with the job and wants to know more about it.

Sense and Sensibility

Anyone can ask questions; however, it takes effort for someone to ask a significant question. That is why job applicants who intend to ask job interviews questions while being interviewed by potential employers should have a reservoir of questions at the back of their heads.

Right timing is also a very important factor in asking questions. You really wouldn't want to ask a far out question that would make your potential employer think that the idea just popped out of nowhere and unplanned. Always remember, right timing is the key to impressive job interviews questions.

Know What You Want to Know

Although sometimes, it may be a bit difficult to formulate questions to ask your interviewer, the secret is to think about what you really want to know about the company or organization. That way, you can exude sincerity when you ask your questions.

The information you gather could actually help you one way or another when you finally get the job. Asking job interviews questions would really help job applicants in landing the job of their dreams because it doesn't only give them an edge above the other applicants, it also gives them the serenity of being able to know the answers to the questions that are bothering them about the job position.

Questions to Ask the Job Interviewer

It is common that during the job interview, you are asked several questions from the employer. At a certain point, you will be given a chance to ask some questions regarding the job you are applying to the interviewer. To gain a good understanding of the company as well as give the impression as a suitable candidate, you need to be prepared with smart questions. Here is a list of questions to pop during the interview.

1. What qualities do you expect the new hires to possess?

By asking this question, it is shown that you are not only concerned about yourself, but also about the job you are applying. By recognizing the necessary quality the new candidate must possess, you agree to work according to the company's standard.

2. What is the typical work day in the position?

This question shows that instead of only thinking about the interview, you have started to envision what kind of responsibilities you will have to perform. This will be an additional point for you as not all candidates have this quality. Most people focus on how to get the job before seriously thinking about how to do the job itself.

3. How long did the previous person in this post hold his/her position? How is the general turnover in the job?

This is your guide to find out if the position is promising. If nobody had stayed in the position for a long duration, it might be a sign that there is something wrong. The problems may vary from unpromising career opportunity to uncooperative colleagues.

4. How is success in this post measured?

The line shows that similar to the manager; you are visualizing what you will need to contribute to the company in order to be succeeded. You will also give the impression that you are a person who will do his or her best to achieve the goal. Answers from the employer will show you what kind of skills and responsibilities are valued most within the job description.

5. How is the work environment in this company?

It is important to fit yourself in an environment you are most comfortable with. For instance, if the working condition is quite relaxed while you are an aggressive and competitive person, you might not get the stimulation to do your best in the position. On the other hand, if the work culture is very formal while you are on the side of a laid-back person, you might get stressed easily at your job. Difficulties in fitting with the work environment will hinder your personal growth as an employee.

Tips For Acing A Job Interview

Finding a job is tough enough as it is without having to go through harrowing interviews. Here's everything you need to know about nailing your interview so you can get through it stress-free.

1. Start With Knowing Who You Are And What You Want.

It's amazing how many job-seekers flub the easiest of all job interview questions "tell me about yourself." By articulating a short response to this issue, you'll be and more importantly appear more confident.

2. Gather Work Samples.

The time and effort of reviewing your work samples and accomplishments lay an excellent foundation for composing responses to typical interview questions. Once you've gathered all your examples, consider assembling a career portfolio for the interview.

3. Develop And Polish Stories That Demonstrate Excellence.

No matter the type of interview you might face, with a collection of stories that demonstrate your passion, expertise, and accomplishments, you'll be ready. If you don't know where to begin in preparing your anecdotes, start with the SAR (situation-action-results) technique.

4. **Ask What To Expect When You're Invited For The Interview.**

Information is a key to your success, and knowing the type of interview to expect and who will be conducting the interview is crucial to your success. Interviewing strategies and models vary widely from traditional questions to stress interviews.

5. **Use Your Network To Learn More About Employer, Open Position.**

See if any of your network contacts or any of their network connections works for your prospective employer. Learn as much as you can about the organization and job opening. Try to uncover why the position is open.

6. **Conduct Interview Prep And Practice.**

Write out responses to typical interview questions, making certain to provide enough detail to answer the questions accurately. Don't memorize the answers, but do run through them a few times after all, as the saying goes, practice makes perfect.

7. **Take Your Interviewing Skills For A Tryout.**

If this interview is your first in a while or just an enormous one for you get your interview prep to the next level by working with a friend or career expert and conducting a mock interview. Remember to evaluate both your verbal and nonverbal responses. Even better? Consider video is recording the mock interview so you can watch it back yourself.

8. Dress For Success.

It's a bit of a cliche now, but in all cliches there is truth and that truth is that appearance does matter. Your goal is to look the part of someone who already works at the employer's workplace. When in doubt, always err on the conservative side. And it's not just about attire, but personal grooming as well. Learn more in our article, When Job-Hunting: Dress for Success.

9. Bring Extra Copies Of Your Resume To The Interview.

You never know when the hiring manager might misplace your resume or when you will spontaneously get invited to interview with others within the organization. Taking along a few extra copies of your resume is a simple, but smart idea.

10. Plan To Arrive A Bit Early To Interview.

Arriving 10-15 minutes before your interview avoid being any earlier offers several advantages. First, the time allows you to catch your breath, compose yourself, and do any last-minute grooming. Second, it provides time to complete any paperwork. Third, it gives you time to observe the work setting and discern how co-workers treat each other.

11. Greet Everyone You Meet With Respect And A Smile.

When you're interviewing, everyone you speak with matters from the receptionist to the assistant to the hiring manage everyone. A surprising number of job-seekers have had their chances derailed by treating a support-staff member rudely.

12. Shine From The Very Beginning Of The Interview.

Making a great first impression begins with a firm handshake, smile, and eye contact. It's important to show your enthusiasm and confidence in the interview, but if you don't get the interview started correctly, you'll spend too much time trying to dig yourself out of the hole.

13. Excel In The Job Interview.

It is the moment when all your preparation pays off. Using positive nonverbals (good posture, eye contact, smile, loud speaking voice) and strong responses should help propel you through the interview successfully. Remember to stay calm even if thrown by an unexpected question.

14. Close The Interview Strongly.

As the interview winds down, now is the time to ask probing questions (unless you have done so already throughout the interview). Asking questions shows your interest. These issues should come from your research. Finally, always close the interview with a thank-you and a request for information about the next step in the process. Learn more in our article, Questions You Can Ask at the Job Interview.

15. Follow-Up The Interview With Thank-You Note And Keep Following-Up.

Once the interview is over, and you're back home (or at a local hotel), sit down and compose thank-you notes to each person you interviewed with. Besides being a nice touch, a thank-you note gives you a chance to reiterate why you are the perfect candidate for the job and to again stress your interest. Finally, continue to follow up regularly (and professionally) until the position is filled.

16. Get The Interview

Before you can ace your interview, you have actually to get the interview. That means making an impressive resumé and making sure it gets through. Once you're done, don't just send it in with the rest. Use your connections and a bit of ingenuity to beat that computerized system and get your resumé into the right hands. If you don't get the interview, find out why and use that to help you the next time around.

17. Prepare Ahead Of Time

So you've got the interview, but you still have a lot of work to do before you walk into that building. The main reason most people suck at interviews is a lack of preparation. So, find out as much as you can about the company, research the job, and formulate a strategy to stand out in that interview among all the other candidates. Getting a cheat sheet together and studying it can help you out, too.

18. Make A Good First Impression

Your job interview starts the second you walk in the door, so be ready. Practice walking into a room if you have to. But more than anything learn how first impressions work and do everything you can to make a good one: be on time, dress and groom yourself well, and be aware of your body language. Remember, just giving a damn will go a long way in your first impression if you don't want to be there, they'll know.

19. Tackle The Tough Questions

Once you're inside, it's time for the hard part: answering the interview questions. Know the questions you'll be expected to answer backwards and forwards, and do some extra research on answering the really tough ones, like "what is your biggest weakness," "have you ever been fired," "Tell me about a challenge you faced with a coworker," or even just the ever-vague "tell me about yourself."

Most of your answers will probably follow a particular pattern, so when in doubt, fall back on the STAR technique. But most of all: learn why they're asking you each question and tailor your responses to their hidden motives.

20. Ask Some Questions Yourself

Your interviewer shouldn't be the only one asking questions. It is your chance to not only make a good impression but learn a bit more about the job you're applying for. Ask a few issues that will get you beautiful, as well as some items that'll show you whether this is the right job for you. With the right questions prepared, you'll be one step ahead of the competition.

21. Emphasize Your Good Qualities

You'll probably feel the need to be humble but don't. Shameless self-promotion is a good thing in job interviews. In fact, it's the only thing you can do to showcase your good qualities. If you don't have the experience to tout, remember that potential is more valuable than experience: if you can show why you're a promising hire, you're in.

22. Avoid The Common Pitfalls

So you've learned what to do, but it's also important to know what to avoid. Even something as simple as negative body language can sabotage your chances, so make sure you aren't hurting yourself without knowing it. Research the subjects you should avoid and make sure you don't overshare, particularly when it comes to your personal life. As long as you don't raise any red flags, you should be good to go.

23. Recover When Things Go South

Hopefully, with the right preparation, your interview will go smoothly. But, if you end up answering a question terribly or hit an ordinary brick wall (like claims of "overqualification"), learn how to turn the tide quickly so you can get back on sound footing. If you leave the interview thinking the whole thing was a disaster, you can always request a second interview explaining the problems you had, too.

24. Follow Up Afterward

Don't let your interview be the last they hear from you. If you follow up afterward, you'll help them remember who you are, and make sure your resume doesn't fall into the abyss of the forgotten. Send a thank you note after your interview, and a short email, later on, to check in if you haven't heard back. Take into account how you've been communicating with them so far, though, as different modes of communication may be more beneficial. If you have a follow-up interview, be sure to nail that too.

25. If You Don't Get Hired, Find Out Why

Not every interview will be a winner, sadly, even if you do everything right. If you don't get hired, the best thing you can do is find out why and apply that knowledge to your next round of interviews. Look back on your interview and think about what you could have done better, whether it's avoiding the "over qualification" trap or better grammar.

Job Interview Mistakes to Avoid

If you've read one or several of the countless publications about job interviews and how to avoid messing up the interview, you may have some good tips and suggestions.

Most of that information may be just fine. However, there are ten common mistakes made in one fashion or the other. Consider this just the "cliff notes" version.

Avoid These Ten Mistakes

1. Arriving late for your job interview

The one thing you avoid at all costs is being late for your interview. If you're hired, you'll be expected to be on time and your ability to be on time for the interview is often a judgment of whether you'll be late if you're hired.

Some suggestions to prevent tardiness are:

Obtaining through directions to the interview location from the recruiter or hiring manager or the HR representative. When possible inquire further about just how much time to allow to either drive (or use public transportation) to your job interview location from wherever you'll be coming. When it's a big organization or plant setting, find out which building your interview will take place in. Don't forget to ask about parking your car and if the parking is free or paid.

Get phone numbers of the interviewer just in case you need them during your trip to the interview, or should you need to reschedule your interview date/time (illness, family emergency, current work conflicts, etc.)

If at all feasible make a trial trip, by driving to the location for the interview. This includes driving to that location at about the same time during the day that your job interview is planned. This provides you with the best idea of just how much time to allow to get to the interview. This is a good time to also scout out the parking arrangement.

Permit yourself a minimum of a 10-15-minute safety net. It's much better to be early, instead of being late.

When you are running late despite all your planning and best efforts (traffic jam, flat tire, inclement weather, etc.) phone the interviewer so that you can notify her or him that you'll be a little late and include the causes for your delay. See whether you can still be interviewed or if you need to reschedule.

2. Overlooking a last minute personal grooming check.

By arriving early ask for the nearest restroom and look in the mirror so that you can make certain your grooming is still appropriate. Make certain your clothes are straight and neat and comb your hair if needed and if you've eaten recently check your teeth to be sure that you don't have food lodged in your teeth. Remember this is a good time to also take that "pit stop" so you won't have to ask to use the restroom in the middle of interviews.

3. Dressing inappropriately.

No matter what level of job you're interviewing for, your clothes must be clean and neat. For professional positions, men and women must dress professionally and what that means may vary from company to company. For many jobs, well put together informal business clothing will be all you need. This isn't the right time or place for jewelry or clothing that is flamboyant. You wouldn't want anything to draw attention away from focus from your qualifications to do the job. It's best to inquire about proper dress code when setting up the interview appointment. And just in case, it's always best to err on the side of being a little overdressed, vs. underdressed.

4. Being trapped into making casual conversation

Numerous interviews start with a casual conversation to place the two you at ease. No matter what, stay away from topics such as politics and religion. Acceptable subjects for casual discussion include sport or the weather, regardless and if you need any assistance locating the company facility for the job interview. Making comments about photos or other things at the place of work is generally effective. Nevertheless, be sure you are in the actual interviewer's office, instead of in an office just being used for the job interview before you discuss workplace items.

5. Being unable to communicate effectively about your current and prior work background.

Many interviewers are certainly not really experienced, and often a few of the more knowledgeable ones will use your resume as a guideline during a job interview. Be ready to discuss everything in-depth that you've listed on your resume. If you can, rehearse having an interview with an associate or friend. Your practice may not be optimal, but it will sure help you increase your interviewing ability all of which will place you ahead of many of your competitors.

6. Being unfamiliar with the job you are being interviewed for.

The more knowledge you get regarding the job and the organization, more probable it is you'll be able to represent yourself as the solution to meet the employer's needs. When you're in a major job hunt, you ought to have completed considerable company research before getting the interview.

Information sources for could be:

The Internet. Both the company's website and websites focussing on the profession or industry.

The library. Industry magazines or publications like the Occupational Outlook Handbook tend to be helpful.

Networking. Talk to individuals who are acquainted with the actual job or business. Linkedin is a great resource for this. In case you do not know a person with the knowledge you seek, you probably know somebody who knows somebody who has that information. Networking begins with asking them questions, so you shouldn't be reluctant to ask others for information and facts.

7. Failing to pay attention to hints about requirements from the company.

Numerous interviewers begin the job interview by supplying you with an understanding of the business and its needs. Treat these details as a treasure. As soon as you've acquired these details, you'll be able to customize your replies to how you are able to assist them in fulfilling those needs. The company is trying to find somebody to solve their challenges and, if you are able to persuade them that you are capable of doing so, you will end up significantly ahead of your competition.

8. Failing to recognize when to quit speaking.

When you have practiced your interview, you will definitely have the ability to plainly and briefly answer their questions and explain your accomplishments. Avoid rambling replies that will move away from the subject of the job interview. Use the SMART method for structuring your answers. This should be a one to three-minute initial response in most cases.

S = Specific
M = measureable
A = Action oriented
R = Results oriented
T = Time specific

Don't be frightened of silence during the interview and don't try to fill in lulls in the conversation. If you're unsure whether or not the job interviewer has gotten sufficient details from your answer, ask them if your response was sufficient, i.e., "have I given you enough information, or would you like more detail?"

9. Failing to ask insightful questions.

Usually, at the conclusion of the job interview, you'll be asked if you have any questions. Avoid using these times to inquire about benefits or when you might take your very first holiday. The questions you ask need to display your desire for the job. You might want to ask questions like:

The most important long term plans for your company? The most important plans for the position you're interviewing for?

Exactly what do you believe are the most crucial skills needed for this job?

How will you evaluate my progress and my accomplishments in this job?

10. Failing to always use a thank-you/follow-up response.

Attempt to get business cards from every person you interview with and make at least one keynote about what you talked with during interview with that person (use the back of the card), then include a comment about that point in your thank you letter. Emails are OK to use. The interviewer's email should be on the business card.

A thank you! Correspondence has several excellent points.

It's going to help remind the interviewer of both you and your qualifications. Very few people really send this sort of correspondence and submitting one should cause you to differentiate yourself. You can use it to add to the responses you presented during your interview. You could strengthen areas in places you thought you failed to thoroughly explain during your interview.

It is possible to add more details - the points you "wish you'd have stated" during the job interview. This could even include a document or white paper or a link on the web that points to what you've done.

All through the job interview process, remember that the process is actually a competition. It's not necessary to be perfect, just superior to the competition. By eliminating these ten ways to mess up a job interview, you will have a high probability of beating your competitors.

Jim Barret

Finish Strong!

The job interview is over. You leave the room and building with a big sigh of relief. You think you've done well, but you never know. You're already thinking out what you have to do for the remaining hours of the day. The job search has been a real learning experience.

Don't get ahead of yourself. You still have some very important things to do to finish strong with this job interview.

If you took notes during the interview and importantly if you didn't take notes now is the time to finish up writing out the content of the interview. Do it as soon as possible, even sitting in your car in the parking lot.

Here are the questions you have to answer. Who did you meet their names and titles? What did they tell you about the job? The most important skills and the least important skills associated with the job? What went well with the interview? Why? What seemed to go poorly? Why? When will you have an answer? Who do you follow-up with? What questions did you ask? What were their answers? Any open issues or concerns? What specific questions were asked? How did you answer? Do you need any improvements in answering questions?

Of immediate concern is to analyze what parts of the interview that you think went poorly. Overall the winning candidate usually gets the job because they have the fewest negatives. Your performance analysis should examine if there are any negatives. Now your challenge is to overcome possible negatives with your thank your letter and hopefully subsequent interviews.

An individual thank you letter should be sent to each person you interviewed with. Each thank you letter should make clear that you understood what was said, you understood the importance of the information provided, and you are excited about the job.

The thank you letter should be sent within one day, and if the decision was going to be made in a couple of days after the interview, send it overnight.

The thank you letter is an additional opportunity to clear up any objections or to add to an answer that needs to be strengthened. Objections not answered means you don't make the sale.

Overall the thank you letter should play back some of the comments made by the interviewer. You recognize the importance of a key skill required in the job. What were you impressed with about the company? Let them know this.

Let them know you are looking forward to the challenges of the position and you are confident you will do well in the position.

Now do something that few do in writing their thank you letters. Ask for the job. Be positive and enthusiastic about the opportunity.

Finally, express appreciation for their time. Now you've finished strong and done everything you can to put you ahead of the other candidates.

One final thing, effective interviewing is a product of experience and preparation. Ask yourself, what can you improve? How are you going to make the next interview better? Acting on the answers to these questions, if for some reason, you do not get the job you just interviewed for will move you over the finish line in your next job interview.

Thanks for choosing this book, make sure to leave a short review on Amazon if you enjoyed it, your opinion is very important for us!

www.ingramcontent.com/pod-product-compliance
Lightning Source LLC
Chambersburg PA
CBHW072223170526
45158CB00002BA/724